FOR THE
Beauty
OF THE
Earth

A COLORING BOOK TO CELEBRATE THE
WONDER OF CREATION

Ink &
Willow

Trade Paperback ISBN 978-0-593-23602-4

Cover design by Nicole Block
Book design by Danielle Deschenes
Cover illustration by Bridget Hurley

Published in the United States by WaterBrook, an imprint of
Random House, a division of Penguin Random House LLC.

Ink & Willow and its colophon are registered trademarks of
Penguin Random House LLC.

Printed in China

2022—First Edition

10 9 8 7 6 5 4 3 2 1

SPECIAL SALES
Most WaterBrook and Ink & Willow books are available at special
quantity discounts when purchased in bulk by corporations, organiza-
tions, and special-interest groups. Custom imprinting or excerpting
can also be done to fit special needs. For information, please email
specialmarketscms@penguinrandomhouse.com.

COLOR YOUR WAY TO A DEEPER APPRECIATION AND LASTING WONDER FOR CREATION

The heavens declare the glory of God;
the skies proclaim the work of his hands.

—*Psalm 19:1*

From snow-capped mountains and deep ocean trenches to lush rainforests and wide-open plains, the earth is full of beauty, variety, and majesty of the most breathtaking yet natural kind. No matter where we might be in the world, testimony of God's amazing creation is never more than a glance away, if only we remember to look. With beautifully designed illustrations and inspiring quotes about the grandeur of nature, this coloring book offers a perfect resource for deepening your appreciation for the natural world and growing in connection with the Creator.

As evidenced by the verse above, Scripture—and in particular the Psalms—are riddled with references to the personification and beauty of creation. On top of that, entire novels, films, and magazines are dedicated to describing and detailing the magic and wonder to be found in the natural world. Countless leaders, speakers, and individuals across the globe are also using their voices to advocate for the preservation and protection of our planet and its resources. In other words, no matter where you might stand on conservation issues or sustainability programs, one truth we can all agree on is that our world is a valuable gift worth appreciating and celebrating.

In her book *Native: Identity, Belonging, and Rediscovering God*, author, speaker, and Potawatomi Nation member Kaitlin B. Curtice wrote,

> *Trees demonstrate community. They understand what it means to care for one another, to care for the whole as they care for themselves. As humans, we are all connected at our root base, and in our struggle to learn what it means to be human to one another and to care for this created world, we are constantly exchanging experiences with one another, good medicine with one another, stories and relationships that are born from the deep well of God.*

So whether you're someone who sees God in a rainbow, is moved to tears by a waterfall, finds rest in a meadow, or can only stand in awe when faced with a mountain, let this coloring book be a source of beauty, inspiration, and deeper union with God as your color your way through its pages.

If you'd like to share some of your artwork and engage with other people using this book, post your finished art on Instagram using the hashtag #FortheBeautyColoringBook.

Doth not all nature around me praise God? If I were silent,
I should be an exception to the universe. Doth not the
thunder praise Him as it rolls like drums in the march of
the God of armies? Do not the mountains praise Him when
the woods upon their summits wave in adoration? Doth
not the lightning write His name in letters of fire? Hath not
the whole earth a voice? And shall I, can I, silent be?

*—Charles Haddon Spurgeon (1834–1892) in "Magnificat,"
a sermon delivered on October 14, 1860. Spurgeon was a preacher
in England and is widely known as the "Prince of Preachers."*

Illustrated by Jennifer Tucker

The best remedy for those who are afraid, lonely or unhappy is to go outside, somewhere where they can be quite alone with the heavens, nature and God. Because only then does one feel that all is as it should be and that God wishes to see people happy, amidst the simple beauty of nature. As longs as this exists, and it certainly always will, I know that then there will always be comfort for every sorrow, whatever the circumstances may be. And I firmly believe that nature brings solace in all troubles.

—*Anne Frank, in* The Diary of a Young Girl, *a classic that details her Jewish family's two years in hiding during the German occupation of the Netherlands. Born in 1929, she died in a German concentration camp in 1945.*

Illustrated by Shannon Contreras

The blue of the sky, the taste of honey, the delicious embrace of water.

C.S. Lewis

"The angels," he said, "have no senses; their experience is purely intellectual and spiritual. That is why we know something about God which they don't. There are particular aspects of His love and joy which can be communicated to a created being only by sensuous experience. Something of God which the seraphim can never quite understand flows into us from the blue of the sky, the taste of honey, the delicious embrace of water whether cold or hot, and even from sleep itself."

—C. S. Lewis (1898–1963) in The Grand Miracle: And Other Selected Essays on Theology and Ethics from God (Ballantine, 1970). Lewis was a professor and renowned Christian writer. He's famous for works such as The Screwtape Letters, Mere Christianity, and his children's series The Chronicles of Narnia.

Illustrated by Laura Marshall Denny

Look deep, deep into nature, and then you will
understand everything better.

—Words from Albert Einstein (1879–1955) to his
stepdaughter Margot, after his sister Maja died in 1951

Illustrated by Jennifer Tucker

I've always regarded nature as the clothing of God.

– Alan Hovhaness

I've always regarded nature as the clothing of God.

—Alan Hovhaness. Hovhaness (1911–2000), born Alan Vaness Chakmakjian, was an Armenian American composer. As a child, Hovhaness developed a love of mountains through his long walks in the hills of New England. That love remained with him throughout his life, working its way into titles of some of his musical works, and the locale of his various homes.

Illustrated by Holly Camp

Look at that sea... all silver and shadow and vision of things not seen.

LUCY MAUD MONTGOMERY

Look at that sea, girls—all silver and shadow and vision
of things not seen. We couldn't enjoy its loveliness any
more if we had millions of dollars and ropes of diamonds.

*—Lucy Maud Montgomery (1874–1942) in Anne of Green
Gables (Puffin, 1994). Montgomery is a Canadian novelist who
grew up on Prince Edward Island.*

Illustrated by Bridget Hurley

Adopt the pace of Nature. Her Secret is patience.

RALPH WALDO EMERSON

Adopt the pace of Nature. Her secret is patience.

—Ralph Waldo Emerson (1803–1882) in "Education" in The Complete Works of Ralph Waldo Emerson: Lectures and Biographical Sketches *(Houghton Mifflin Company, 1911). Emerson was an American poet, essayist, and philosopher.*

Illustrated by Jennifer Tucker

He has made
everything
beautiful
in its time

–Ecclesiastes 3:11

He has made everything beautiful in its time. He has also
set eternity in the human heart; yet no one can fathom
what God has done from beginning to end.

—*Ecclesiastes 3:11*

Illustrated by Holly Camp

Praise Him all creatures here below.

· Thomas Ken ·

Praise God from Whom All Blessings Flow

Praise God, from whom all blessings flow;
Praise Him, all creatures here below;
Praise Him above, ye heav'nly host;
Praise Father, Son, and Holy Ghost.
Amen.

—Thomas Ken (1637–1711) was an Anglican bishop and hymn writer. In 1673, he wrote three hymns for students at Winchester College that he wanted them to sing daily. Each of these closed with these four familiar lines we now know as the Doxology.

Illustrated by Ann-Margret Hovsepian

In the beginning God created the heavens and the earth. GENESIS 1:1

In the beginning God created the heavens and the earth. Now the earth was formless and empty, darkness was over the surface of the deep, and the Spirit of God was hovering over the waters.

And God said, "Let there be light," and there was light. God saw that the light was good, and he separated the light from the darkness. God called the light "day," and the darkness he called "night." And there was evening, and there was morning—the first day.

—Genesis 1:1–5

Illustrated by Bridget Hurley

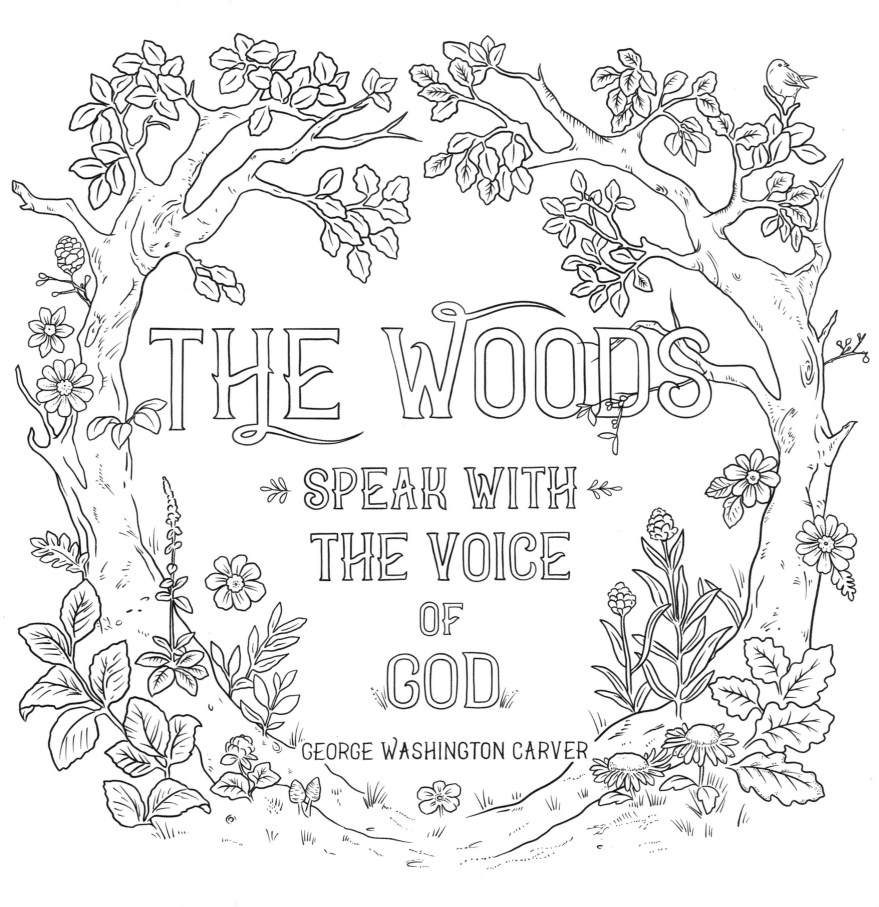

Reading about nature is fine, but if a person walks in the woods and listens carefully, he can learn more than what is in books, for they speak with the voice of God.

—George Washington Carver, in The Essential Writings of the American Black Church (AMG, 2008). Carver (1864–1943), born into slavery a year before it was outlawed, became a prominent Black agricultural scientist who developed hundreds of products using peanuts, sweet potatoes, and soybeans.

Illustrated by Shannon Contreras

the whole world is a series of miracles
– HANS CHRISTIAN ANDERSEN –

The whole world is a series of miracles ... but we're so accustomed to them that we call them every-day matters.

—Hans Christian Andersen (1805–1875) in "The Puppet Showman." Andersen was a Danish author, famous for his fairy tales, many of which are still well-known today, such as "The Princess and the Pea" and "Thumbelina."

Illustrated by Laura Marshall Denny

For after all, the best thing one can do
When it is raining, is to let it rain.

——Henry Wadsworth Longfellow (1807–1882) in "The Poet's Tale:
The Birds of Killingworth." Longfellow was an American poet and scholar,
known for his translation of Dante's The Divine Comedy.

Illustrated by Jennifer Tucker

The woods
are lovely,
dark and deep.

ROBERT FROST

The woods are lovely, dark and deep.
But I have promises to keep,
and miles to go before I sleep.

—Robert Frost (1874–1963) in "Stopping by Woods on a Snowy Evening" in New Hampshire: A Poem with Notes and Grace Notes *(Henry Holt & Company, 1923). Frost was an American poet. One of his most well-known poems is "The Road Not Taken."*

Illustrated by Natasha Donovan

We need to find God and God cannot be found in noise
    and restlessness. God is the friend of silence.
See how nature—trees and flowers and grass grow in
    silence.
See the stars, the moon and the sun, how they move in
    silence.

—Mother Teresa (1910–1997) in The Joy in Loving *(Penguin Compass,
1996). Mother Teresa was a nun and missionary who served the poor and
destitute around the world. She has been honored by the Roman Catholic
church as Saint Teresa of Calcutta.*

Illustrated by Ann-Margret Hovsepian

Love of nature is a common language
— Jimmy Carter

Like music and art, love of nature is a common language
that can transcend political or social boundaries.

—Jimmy Carter in An Outdoor Journal (University of Arkansas
Press, 1994). Carter (born in 1924) was the thirty-ninth president
of the United States of America.

Illustrated by Holly Camp

Look at that beautiful butterfly, and learn from it to
trust in God. One might wonder where it could live in
tempestuous nights, in the whirlwind, or in the stormy
day; but I have noticed it is safe and dry under the broad
leaf while rivers have been flooded, and the mountain
oaks torn up from their roots.

*—Jeremy Taylor (1613–1667) was an Anglican bishop and writer. Known for
his poetic flair, Taylor has been called the "Shakespeare of Divines."*

Illustrated by Shannon Contreras

The mountains are calling and I must go.

—John Muir (1838–1914) in Our National Parks (Houghton Mifflin, 1901).
Muir was born in Scotland and immigrated to the United States in 1849.
A naturalist and explorer, his writings helped lead to the creation of the
following national parks: Yosemite, Sequoia, Grand Canyon, and Mount Rainier.

Illustrated by Bridget Hurley

A BIRD, A FRUIT ON A TREE, A FLOWER, WATCHING A RIVER FLOW... IT IS *refreshing* TO KNOW THAT LIFE IS *everywhere.*

Wangari Maathai

Give yourself time to think and find your direction
once again; allow your own reserves of energy to be
replenished through time in the natural world. You don't
have to have a particular place of solace in nature.
Perhaps you feel the need to disappear into a forest or a
cave, but a park or just sitting on a riverbank can serve,
too. In fact, anything can capture our attention: a bird, a
fruit on a tree, a flower, watching a river flow; just being
quiet. It is refreshing to know that life is everywhere.

——Wangari Maathai (1940–2011) in Replenishing the Earth
*(Doubleday, 2010). Maathai was a scholar and human rights activist
and the first African woman to win the Nobel Peace Prize.*

Illustrated by Ann-Margret Hovsepian

Through Him all things were made

JOHN 1:3

Through him all things were made; without him nothing
was made that has been made.

—*John 1:3*

Illustrated by Laura Marshall Denny

I'LL ACQUAINT MYSELF WITH THE GLACIERS AND WILD GARDENS, AND GET AS NEAR THE HEART OF THE WORLD AS I CAN.

John Muir

As long as I live, I'll hear waterfalls and birds
and winds sing. I'll interpret the rocks, learn the language
of flood, storm, and the avalanche. I'll
acquaint myself with the glaciers and wild gardens,
and get as near the heart of the world as I can.

—*John Muir (1838–1914) in* To Yosemite and Beyond *(University of Utah, 1999). Muir was born in Scotland and immigrated to the United States in 1849. A naturalist and explorer, his writings helped lead to the creation of the following national parks:* Yosemite, Sequoia, Grand Canyon, and Mount Rainier.

Illustrated by Natasha Donovan

In his hand is the life of every creature.

JOB 12:7-10

But ask the animals, and they will teach you,
    or the birds in the sky, and they will tell you;
or speak to the earth, and it will teach you,
    or let the fish in the sea inform you.
Which of all these does not know
    that the hand of the Lord has done this?
In his hand is the life of every creature
    and the breath of all mankind.

—Job 12:7–10

Illustrated by Jennifer Tucker

All *created* *things* ARE TRULY *Sacred* IN THEIR *beginnings*

KAITLIN B. CURTICE

We must work together, across every divide, and
the church must be willing to step into really difficult
conversations for the sake of a better future for all things
and everyone. Maybe that begins with recognizing that
all created things are truly sacred in their beginnings, and
maybe then we can truly begin to dismantle systems of
oppression.

—*Kaitlin B. Curtice, in* Native: Identity, Belonging, and
Rediscovering God *(Brazos, 2020). A member of the Potawatomi
Nation, she is a poet, writer, and professor.*

Illustrated by Shannon Contreras

Nature takes its course from God; therefore she is an art from God, that is His natural order and procession; and that which proceeds from Nature, and follows it, we may say is a child of Nature: natural art proceeds from Nature, and follows it as a pupil does a master.

——Dante Alighieri (1265–1321) in The Inferno. *Dante was a renowned Italian poet, writer, and philosopher, best known for his epic poem* La commedia *(now known as* The Divine Comedy*).*

Illustrated by Ann-Margret Hovsepian

God writes His Gospel not in the Bible alone, but in trees, and flowers, and clouds, and stars.

MARTIN LUTHER

God writes His Gospel not in the Bible alone, but in trees, and flowers, and clouds, and stars.

—Martin Luther (1483–1546) in Watchwords for the Warfare of Life (T. Nelson and Sons, 1869). Luther was a German theologian and religious reformer. A prominent figure of the sixteenth century Protestant Reformation, he's one of the most influential figures in Christian history.

Illustrated by Jennifer Tucker

Not all those who wander are lost.

—J. R. R. Tolkien (1892–1973) in The Fellowship of the Ring
(HarperCollins, 1991). Tolkien was an English fantasy writer and scholar.
He's best known for The Hobbit and the Lord of the Rings series.

Illustrated by Holly Camp

For the beauty
of the earth, for the
glory of the skies.

FOLLIOTT S. PIERPOINT

For the Beauty of the Earth

For the beauty of the earth,
For the glory of the skies,
For the love which from our birth
Over and around us lies—

Lord of all, to Thee we raise
This our hymn of grateful praise.

For the wonder of each hour
Of the day and of the night,
Hill and vale, and tree and flow'r,
Sun and moon, and stars of light,

Lord of all, to Thee we raise
This our hymn of grateful praise.

For the joy of human love,
Brother, sister, parent, child,
Friends on earth and friends above,
For all gentle thoughts and mild—
Lord of all, to Thee we raise
This our hymn of grateful praise.

—Folliott S. Pierpoint (1835–1917) was an English hymnodist, poet, and schoolmaster. "For the Beauty of the Earth" is his most famous hymn.

Illustrated by Bridget Hurley

They praised the morning, gloried in the sea, sympathized in the delight of the fresh-feeling breeze.

Jane Austen

They praised the morning; gloried in the sea;
sympathized in the delight of the fresh-feeling
breeze—and were silent.

—Jane Austen (1775–1817) in Persuasion *(Penguin Classics,
2006). Austen was a English writer, famous for her novels,
including* Pride and Prejudice *and* Emma.

Illustrated by Ann-Margret Hovsepian

My favorite
color has
always
been sunset.

MATTIE J. T. STEPANEK

My favorite color
Has always been sunset—
Pink and orange swirled
With purple, gray, and brown.

—*Mattie J.T. Stepanek (1990–2004) in "Color Choice," a poem in* Reflections of a Peacemaker *(Andrews McMeel Publishing, 2005). Stepanek was an American poet and an advocate of peace. He wrote seven bestselling books of poetry and peace essays before his death at the young age of thirteen.*

Illustrated by Natasha Donovan

I cannot endure to waste anything so precious as autumnal sunshine by staying in the house.

• NATHANIEL HAWTHORNE •

I cannot endure to waste anything so precious as autumnal sunshine by staying in the house.

—*Nathaniel Hawthorne (1804–1864) in* Passages from the American Note-Books *(Houghton, Mifflin, and Company, 1886). Hawthorne was an American novelist and short-story writer. A master of allegory, he's known for his novels* The Scarlet Letter *and* The House of the Seven Gables.

Illustrated by Laura Marshall Denny

God clothes
the grass
of the field

Matthew 6:28-30

And why do you worry about clothes? See how the flowers of the field grow. They do not labor or spin. Yet I tell you that not even Solomon in all his splendor was dressed like one of these. If that is how God clothes the grass of the field, which is here today and tomorrow is thrown into the fire, will he not much more clothe you— you of little faith?

—Matthew 6:28–30

Illustrated by Holly Camp

The earth is what we all have in common.

—Wendell Berry, in The Art of the Commonplace (Counterpoint, 2002). Born in 1934, Berry is a writer and farmer and has published more than eighty books of poetry, fiction, and essays.

Illustrated by Ann-Margret Hovsepian

How many are your works, Lord!
   In wisdom you made them all;
   the earth is full of your creatures.
There is the sea, vast and spacious,
   teeming with creatures beyond number—
   living things both large and small.

—Psalm 104:24–25

Illustrated by Jennifer Tucker

Between every two pines is a doorway to a new world.

—John Muir (1838–1914). A naturalist and explorer, Muir was born in Scotland and immigrated to the United States in 1849. His writings helped lead to the creation of the following national parks: Yosemite, Sequoia, Grand Canyon, and Mount Rainer.

Illustrated by Shannon Contreras

He holds in his hands the depths of the earth
and the mightiest mountains.
The sea belongs to him, for he made it.
His hands formed the dry land, too.

—Psalm 95:4–5 (NLT)

Illustrated by Laura Marshall Denny

For you shall go out in joy
and be led forth in peace;
the mountains and the hills before you
shall break forth into singing,
and all the trees of the field shall clap their hands.

—Isaiah 55:12 (ESV)

Illustrated by Bridget Hurley

7-24-2023

The Creator is calling us
back to experience God's
love and care in the
created world around us.

Randy Woodley

The Creator is calling us back to experience God's love
and care in the created world around us.

—Randy Woodley in Shalom and the Community of Creation:
*An Indigenous Vision (Eerdmans, 2012). Woodley, a Keetoowah
Cherokee Indian descendent, is a theologian, author, and professor.*

Illustrated by Holly Camp

Nature must be respected and preserved

Richard Twiss

The Western industrialized world and postmodern society failed to realize until it was almost too late that nature must be respected and preserved. As far back as can be traced, Indian people have been aware of this need. For the most part, Native people have respected nature, killing only what they needed for food, clothing or shelter. Natives believe the land was created by God and, hence, is sacred, while Western culture views land as a natural resource or commodity.

—Richard Twiss (1954– 2013), in One Church, Many Tribes (Chosen, 2000). Twiss, a member of the Sicangu Lakota Oyate from the Rosebud Sioux Reservation in South Dakota, was an educator and author. Desiring to bring the gospel to Native Americans, Twiss cofounded Wiconi International.

Illustrated by Shannon Contreras

You made
the EARTH and
the SEAS and
EVERYTHING
in them.

Nehemiah 9:6

You alone are the LORD. You made the skies and the
heavens and all the stars. You made the earth and the
seas and everything in them. You preserve them all, and
the angels of heaven worship you.

—Nehemiah 9:6 (NLT)

Illustrated by Ann-Margret Hovsepian

It's AMAZING what a day ON THE WATER can do for the soul.

DORINA LAZO GILMORE-YOUNG

It's amazing what a day on the water can do for the soul.
These are the days of sun-kissed skin, juicy watermelon
cubes, reading fat books, and floating on inner tubes.
Summer, you can't stay forever, but we are grateful for
your visit just the same. These are the days that will fuel
me and remind me what it feels like to be wholly alive.
All glory.

— *From an Instagram post by Dorina Lazo Gilmore-Young,
an author, speaker, Bible teacher, and spoken word artist.*

Illustrated by Jennifer Tucker

I BELIEVE IN US
CARVING OUT OUR OWN
SPACES IN THE WORLD
TO WRITE OUR STORIES.

Tanaya Winder

I believe in us carving out our own spaces in the world to write our stories.

—*Tanaya Winder, a member of the Duckwater Shoshone Tribe, is an author, singer/songwriter, poet, speaker, and educator.*

Illustrated by Natasha Donovan

The LORD is my shepherd, I lack nothing.
    He makes me lie down in green pastures,
he leads me beside quiet waters.

—Psalm 23:1–2

Illustrated by Ann-Margret Hovsepian

You paint
the wayside flower,
you light
the evening star.

MATTHIAS CLAUDIUS

We Plough the Fields, and Scatter

We plough the fields, and scatter
the good seed on the land,
but it is fed and watered
by God's almighty hand.
God sends the snow in winter,
the warmth to swell the grain,
the breezes, and the sunshine,
and soft refreshing rain.

Refrain:
All good gifts around us are sent from heav'n above.
We thank you, God, we thank you, God, for all your love.

You only are the Maker
of all things near and far.
You paint the wayside flower,
you light the evening star.
The winds and waves obey you,
by you the birds are fed;
much more to us, your children,
you give our daily bread. *[Refrain]*

We thank you, then, Creator,
for all things bright and good,
the seed-time, and the harvest,
our life, our health, our food.
Accept the gifts we offer
for all your love imparts,
and what you most would welcome:
our humble, thankful hearts. *[Refrain]*

—Matthias Claudius (1740–1815), translated by Jane M. Campbell.
Claudius, the son of a Lutheran pastor, was a German poet.

Illustrated by Bridget Hurley

MAN'S
HEART
away from nature

BECOMES

HARD

Luther Standing Bear

Wherever forests have not been mowed down, wherever
the animal is recessed in their quiet protection, wherever
the earth is not bereft of four-footed life—that to [the
white man] is an "unbroken wilderness."

But since for the Lakota was no wilderness; since
nature was not dangerous but hospitable; not forbidding
but friendly. . . . Indian faith sought the harmony of man
with his surroundings; the other sought the dominance of
surroundings. . . .

For one man the world was full of beauty; for the
other it was a place of sin and ugliness to be endured
until he went to another world.

But the old Lakota was wise. He knew that man's
heart away from nature becomes hard.

—Luther Standing Bear (1868–1939) in Land of the Spotted Eagle
*(University of Nebraska, 1933). Luther Standing Bear, an Oglala Lakota
chief, was an author, actor, philosopher, and educator.*

Illustrated by Shannon Contreras